Given to Prayer

GIVEN TO PRAYER

CHERYL STASINOWSKY

WORD SCRIBE

GIVEN TO PRAYER
Copyright © 2015 by Cheryl Stasinowsky

All rights reserved. No part of this book may be reproduced, stored in a retrieval system, or transmitted in any form or by any means-electronic, mechanical, photocopy, recording, or otherwise-without prior written permission of the copyright owner, except by a reviewer who wishes to quote brief passages in connection with a review for inclusion in a magazine, website, newspaper, podcast, or broadcast. Cheryl Stasinowsky does not capitalize the name of satan or any reference to the devil.

All Scripture quotations, unless otherwise indicated, are taken from the New King James Version of the Bible. Copyright © 1982 by Thomas Nelson, Inc.

Interior design and cover design provided by www.truenorthpublish.com.

Published by WordScribe.

ISBN: 978-0692629680

For Worldwide Distribution. Published in the United States of America.

Dedication

I dedicate this book to my children. I have prayed for you every day of your life. I dedicate this book to my grandchildren and all generations after that. I might not ever meet you in person, but I want you to know that I am praying for you now. I am that praying grandma and great-grandma. I want you all to know that I have prayed into your future. I have not just lived focused on today, but have placed prayers ahead of you. I leave you my faith and prayers and I want you to know that I love you and am thinking about you even now ...

My Family

I am "Given to Prayer" for them

Table of Contents

Acknowledgements
Endorsements
Introduction

Chapter 1: My Prayer Journey 21
Chapter 2: Learning to Hear 27
Chapter 3: It's a Conversation 35
Chapter 4: Talking with Whom? 39
Chapter 5: What Does He Do? 45
Chapter 6: Practical Intercession 49
Chapter 7: Teach Us How to Pray 51
Chapter 8: Jesus Prays 57
Chapter 9: Prayer that Changes Me 61
Chapter 10: Awareness Awakened 65
Chapter 11: Praying for Others 69
Chapter 12: Parents 77
Chapter 13: Hindrances to Prayer 83
Chapter 14: Prayers of Faith or Fear? 89
Chapter 15: Extras 93

Do You Need Jesus?
About the Author
More Titles by Cheryl Stasinowsky

Acknowledgements

Father, Son, and Holy Spirit

This book is evidence of Your work in me. Nothing in this book would even be possible or part of my life without You. You have personally taught me exceedingly and abundantly above all that I could ask or think. I love talking to You. I know You listen. I greatly appreciate Your constant availability to be in communication with me. I love You!

My Husband, Wally

I love you more every day. We have walked through so very much together. Some of the things that you have allowed me to experience in God have been such a rich blessing to me. Thank you for allowing me to learn, experience, and grow in God. It has been a wild ride, and it will continue until death do us part. I love you!

Amber and Daniel

I love you both! I put much prayer into your meeting and marriage. It was worth every moment to see you both grow and learn to walk out life together. I will not stop praying for you both, together and individually. You will see generations that I will only get to pray for. What an honor to be a part of your lives. I love you!

Jordan

Son, I love you! I have prayed for you since you were born and even before that. I will continue to pray for you as long as I am alive. I love who you are becoming and who you are right now. Thank you for being my son. It is such an honor to be called your mom. I will always be there to listen, help, love, and pray for you. I love you!

Jean

Wow, another book. Every book I write is so much better after you go through and clean it up. I never knew so many commas were necessary. I love your little notes in the editing that always make me smile. May the Lord richly bless you for all the hours upon hours of reading and re-reading that you do. You are a brilliant and humble editor that I could not do without. Thank you!

Brian

Here we are, another book. You are wonderful to work with. I love how you listen to my visions for each book, and then, somehow, make it happen. You never complain or argue with me. You are a valuable asset to this team to make these books happen. Thank you!

Friends and Family

Thank you for all of your love, encouragement, and support over the years. It is a pleasure to write for you and share what I have learned. My books would go nowhere without you. Thank you for reading and sharing these books with your friends. I am forever grateful to all of you!

Endorsements

The Bible talks about a great cloud of witnesses. I believe that we have a crowd of witnesses here on earth. As Cheryl takes us in depth on how to pray, I am one of her witnesses. Cheryl is my wife of 33 years and I can attest that what she writes is pure and true. I have walked out many of these stories with her. I am still in awe to how she can take a situation that is going bad, or has gone bad, and turns it into good, or how she loves the unlovable. I still, to this day, learn from her revelation and perspective. Cheryl is the real deal! Read this book! I couldn't put it down...

Thank you, Cheryl, for loving me.

Wally Stasinowsky
California

I have had the honor and privilege to read all of Cheryl's books, and like the others, "Given to Prayer" is another excellent book. Her heart for Jesus shows through as she journeys through her process of learning to hear from God and her conversations with Him while in prayer.

I love how she takes you on her journey through many of her life experiences, and how she grew through each one through her daily prayer life and walk with God. Her honesty in revealing that sometimes she is distracted from prayer made me reevaluate places that may be distracting me as well. Her life changing encounters with Him drew me through each chapter hungry and expectant to what I would learn and apply to my daily prayer life.

Each chapter is filled with ways to grow in your prayer life and relationship with our Heavenly Father. Cheryl breaks down the Lord's Prayer showing us how to apply it as a model and guide when approaching God. She also clearly teaches that when we pray for others, we position that person to have an encounter with Jesus. Her book made me want to pray for others without fear, and instead, faith in knowing that our prayers are powerful and life changing through the Holy Spirit.

I highly recommend this book. It has had a profound effect on my prayer life already. It's wonderfully written, practical and encouraging. I believe that as you read it, you will find yourself stopping to pray and putting into practice everything that you have learned. I feel that my prayer life has been re-ignited and that my relationship with the Lord will grow deeper and closer by being given to prayer. Thank you, Cheryl, for sharing your heart and soul with us and future generations that will surely be blessed by your wonderful books.

Caron Ann Quaid
California

Yea, Cheryl! You did it again! Another great book--a great teaching tool for those who want to get serious about a deeper, more meaningful prayer life. Thank you, Cheryl, for your willingness to share your personal trials and victories that others might learn from your experiences and become given to prayer.

Jean Hudak Kashella
Pennsylvania

I have not known Cheryl for long. I only know her through our Facebook networking. A post she made caught my eye when I needed it...Un-forgiveness. Even though I am not acquainted with her personally, I do know the God she is writing about. Ruth left the land of familiarity to know the God that gave Naomi strength in her tragedies. What gives a person such hope that God will turn things around for them?! Given to Prayer does just that. It brings clarity, desire and the need for that hope, a deeper conversation with God to bring that hope into perspective in any situation. You can't take away from a person what they know. In prayer, what you speculate, question, lose sleep over and ignore is all bought to that point of facing it with the One who can bring clarity and an answer. Cheryl has penned a tool that will bring prayer strategy to many believers and non believers. She is "handing her faith" to many generations. Yes, there may be a lot of books out on prayer, but not all of them will be coming from a personal place. I can see this becoming a group bible study or a personal devotion to a new believer or someone who has kept the faith but needs to understand the breakdown of communication between them and God. She has given herself to prayer and presented you with the private moments even as

Jesus did, to bring us closer to our Father. I encourage you as you read to say, "Father let my journey to You begin again with fresh eyes and childlike faith and belief that you are truly Abba Father, consistently there to hear my cry."

Stephanie K. Scott
Virginia

Men, this book is for you. It may be short, but it is power packed. Cheryl is candid and relevant, sharing struggles that we have been through in our own journey. It is engaging, so you might read it in one sitting, but then you will want to reread it. It provides hope, builds faith, and is downright practical. It will call you to a deeper walk with the Lord, equip you to overcome obstacles, and impart resolve to press on to greater victory in your prayers. You will, very likely, think of several people with whom you want to share it.

Rev. Peter A. Carlson
Is. 40:31
Oregon

Introduction

As I sat going through all of the chapters in this book, I became in awe of a faithful God. I am amazed at what He has brought me through and taught me. I am in awe of His creativity in showing me. Through all of my struggles of life over the last 13 plus years, He has taught me about Him, and that He is dependable, trustworthy, faithful, truthful, helpful, understanding, wise, and always knows what to do. I have learned that nothing in my life is impossible to Him.

I am now 54 years old, and I have only discovered what is in this book over the last 13 plus years. I became a Christian at the age of 17, and did not have a clue how to pray. I did not understand prayer. I saw prayer as a duty of what you were supposed to do. I knew I was supposed to thank Him and ask Him for things, but to really have a conversation with the God of all creation… well, that never connected for me until I encountered the Holy Spirit.

My relationship with the Father, the Son, and the Holy Spirit is real, but it has been a journey of learning. I have learned over the years that He wants to communicate with us, and He always is; we just need to learn how He does it. I am real in this book. I talk about my own personal struggles with prayer. I love to pray now, but I have not always loved it.

This is not a book on formulas to pray better. This is a book filled with my own personal journey in learning how He communicates with me. I share thoughts, struggles, victories, and defeats. I do not profess to have prayer all figured out. I think it is a life-long discovery for each individual. I have good days and tough days. I have times where prayer and communication with God is easy, and days when I wonder where He is.

I have shared, to the best of my ability, what I have learned, and hope that it breaks off lies, gives new and fresh insight, and helps to bring understanding to some of the struggles common to all of us, and most of all, that all will come to discover how faithful He truly is to each of us.

My prayer for this book is that relationships with the Father, the Son, and the Holy Spirit will be restored, strengthened, and enriched. My heart is to help others in their own journey of prayer, and that generations will be changed because of prayer. I hope that all will feel encouraged to begin, continue, or even start again talking to God. I pray that after reading this book, you will find Him more real and personal than you find Him right now while reading this introduction. I hope I introduce you to the most amazing relationship with God through prayer. I pray you will pick up helpful tools and insight. My heart is to give you what I have learned so you can take and apply it to enhance prayer in your life. I pray He speaks to you in this book. I pray you have an encounter with God. May the words on these pages speak deeply to you ...

I do not want this just to be another book on prayer; there are plenty of them. I want this book to be "prayer" life-changing encounter for everyone who reads it. May the impossible become possible. May the distant become close ... May a new life of prayer and talking to God open up to you. I love who I get to talk to each moment of my life. I trust Him. I have learned His availability, and I pray you do, too. May prayer be natural.

I am given to prayer. It is what I do, who I am, and how I think. I love it. It is amazing. I pray this will be your testimony, as well ...

While I was writing this book, I listened to a playlist on my iPod. I like to make my own greatest hits, and I put all of my favorite worship music in one place and listen to it repeatedly until it stops ministering to me. In case you want to do that while you read this book, here is my list ...

Who Can Compare? *By Mary Kat Ehrenzeller*

We Dance *By Bethel Music & Steffany Frizzell Gretzinger*

Draw Near *(feature Jeremy Riddle) Bethel Music*

Amazed *By Ross Parsley*

Still Believe *By Kim Walker-Smith*

Glory Come Down *By Derek Johnson*

Oceans *By Hillsong UNITED*

Future/Past *By John Mark McMillan*

Beautiful *By Kari Jobe*

Revelation Song *By Kari Jobe*

You Don't Miss a Thing *By Bethel Music & Amanda Cook*

Ever Be *By Bethel Music & Kalley Heiligenthal*

Enjoy!!

"I take my prayer closet with me on the plane, in the car, or walking down the street. I pray always. My life is prayer."

— Kathryn Kuhlman

(Agreed and Given to by Cheryl Stasinowsky)

CHAPTER 1
My Prayer Journey

For about the first 19 years of my Christian life, my journey with prayer was a struggle. I cannot say I thought of it that way, but it was very weak. I was very busy with life and raising two children, running a construction business, and everything else life had to offer. I went to church and would bow my head and pray, but to spend any length of time in prayer or pray out loud...did not happen very often.

I was a list person, so I created a prayer list for each day of the week. I broke it down and had about 5 items to pray for each day. I cannot say I always got to them, but it was a target. I did, however, pray for my kids every day, and also, for their future spouse. I would pray for my husband and our business, and for whatever issue was happening with a client at the time. But it was hit and miss, and more of a ritual than a relationship.

Some time ago, before my encounter with the Holy Spirit, having been on the church board, I was required to attend a prayer time before the morning services. The attendees were all sitting on the floor, heads bowed, praying. I was trying to stay focused but had no intention of praying aloud. This one particular Sunday, a visitor was in attendance, and when she began to pray, she got my attention. As she prayed, I wondered how she could pray like that. I was in awe of her prayer. There was definitely something different in her praying, and secretly, I wanted to be able to pray like that.

My personal prayer life after the Holy Spirit encounter was very rich, and I spent hours talking to God. We talked and talked. I enjoyed every second of it. I got to know Him and He taught me things, and I would ask Him questions. I loved hanging out with Him.

After my encounter with the Holy Spirit, our church was having a time of prayer every morning at 6:00 A.M. for six weeks prior to Easter. I felt the Lord wanted me to attend. So, I got up every morning and drove the 20 minutes to this one-hour time of prayer. Each day, I simply listened. They all knew how to pray like the lady that one morning several years prior. I was so intimidated that in no way was I going to pray aloud. Day after day I left discouraged. I had things to pray about, but I just did not have the courage to speak it. Interesting that I would then hear someone else pray what I wanted to pray. When the Holy Spirit is guiding the prayers, He makes sure they get prayed by someone.

As I attended each day, I learned a lot. The Lord was teaching me how to pray, not in how they did it, but in gaining confidence that what I was hearing was to be prayed. It happened day after day. One morning, I had something I wanted to pray about, but their prayers were so long and mine seemed so short, I could not get up the courage to pray aloud. I told that to the Lord. All of a sudden, everyone was praying short prayers. I was shocked, so I got up the courage and said my little prayer. I left feeling encouraged that I finally prayed.

On the last morning of this 6-week time of prayer, the Lord gave me a vision of what He wanted me to do at the prayer time. I really did not want to do it because what He was showing me had not been done during the entire 6 weeks...I was so afraid to do it. I kept wrestling with Him the whole prayer time. I was so distracted by what He wanted me to do that I did not hear what anyone else was saying. I kept watching the clock as time ticked away. I felt the Lord really pressing on me to do what He showed me to do. I was fighting Him so strongly and He was fighting me so strongly that I stood up and, out loud, said, "Okay, I give up. I will pray." I explained what the Lord wanted me to do and they all agreed that I could. I went to each leader of our church and prayed over them. I am not sure what happened but something broke, and I felt so empowered to pray. I left that meeting totally different. I was no longer afraid to pray aloud. I do not know what I prayed, but I really prayed from heaven and God showed up. On the last day, in the last few minutes, I submitted to Him and everything changed.

Soon, I was praying for people, over people, and interceding all the time. My public prayer life totally changed. People love to have me pray for them; they tell me that. It is a little weird to me, but I do love to pray and I love and trust the One I am talking to. To me, there is nothing better than discovering what heaven wants prayed on earth and speaking it into existence. It is like I go somewhere else and I feel so empowered and close to the Lord that I do not want to stop.

It has been quite a journey. He has helped me greatly. The empowerment of the Holy Spirit was the key for me. I have learned over the years how to partner with the Holy Spirit. Most of the time, when I pray for someone, I do not want to know what they want prayer for, because I want the Holy Spirit to show me how to pray. I have discovered that when I do this and the Holy Spirit reveals what is going on when they did not tell me, their faith grows and they receive because they know I did not know. At the beginning it was a little scary, but I trust Him fully now.

Yes, I do find times where it is hard to pray for someone. I have prayed for someone to be raised from the dead and they did not come back to life. I have prayed for the sick and I did not see them get better, and they have even died. I have a history now of times it did not work out as I had prayed, but it hasn't stopped me. Yes, I have to pick myself up, but I keep praying.

One time, I was speaking at a church in Uganda. I felt so anointed as I preached the message. At the end of the message I asked if there was anyone who wanted prayer. Every single person in that small church came forward for prayer. As I prayed, I felt nothing. The anointing lifted and I kept praying but felt nothing. They did not speak the same language as I did, and the interpreter was not interpreting the prayers. I had no idea if anything was happening or not. I went back to my hotel room that night quite discouraged. I asked the Lord what happened. He began to explain Hebrews 11:1, "Now faith is the substance of things hoped for, the evidence of things not seen." I was looking with my physical eyes for the evidence and it could not be seen. He explained that I was taking the substance of my faith and joining it with theirs, and He was imparting to them greater faith. What I pray for is not about me and it is not my responsibility to make it happen, it is His. I got it. I was grateful for the revelation.

The next night, after teaching, the pastor told me I had just given a healing message and I needed to have everyone come forward who needed healing. Inside I was thinking...no way, I cannot do that. He insisted. So, I gave the call and 22 people came forward for healing. Yikes! I remembered the revelation and focused on the fact that I could not heal one of these people on my own. Only He could heal them. It was not about me. I prayed with the interpreter this time and had her ask what was wrong; I know what I said earlier but this was different. I prayed for the first person and they just walked away. I asked the interpreter to ask them why they walked away. They said that they were healed. I found it hard to believe and pressed them harder. I wanted to make sure that they were real about this and they were. I prayed for the next person and God healed them. Person after person received healing. The final test came when a woman was holding a crying baby. The baby was very sick and had been for days. So, I prayed and got out of my fears and self, knowing that this baby was not going to know how to pretend. God healed that baby and he stopped crying. Then the mom wanted prayer and God healed her. He taught me a valuable lesson that time in Uganda.

So, He has taken me off on a journey of personal prayer and conversation, praying for others aloud, praying for the sick, interceding for others, and all the while, I was growing in my confidence, trust and relationship with the Father, Jesus, and the Holy Spirit. It has evolved and grown. It was not easy, but worth it. It is the most wonderful part of my faith. I love to talk to the Father, Jesus, and the Holy Spirit. I speak to each of Them at different times. I have journeyed into a relationship with each of Them...

CHAPTER 2
Learning to Hear

As I look back over the last thirteen years, I can see the Lord teaching me over and over how to hear His voice. We all want to hear His voice, and one of the many things I am asked is, "How do I hear His voice like you do?" I do not know the answer to this question. I have come to understand that we are all different and He speaks to each of us individually. I can say He speaks to me this way or that way, and yet, He may never communicate that way to another. Hearing His voice is as individual as each of us. We are not made to look the same, so why would we be made to hear the same? Even the four Gospels do not give an exact account of the life of Jesus. We all place value on different things and focus on the areas that we personally value. He knows that, and He knows exactly how to speak to us uniquely so we hear Him. We just need to learn how He speaks to us...

I did go through an intense season of learning, although I think every season is intense as we are being stretched beyond what we see and believe, to hear His voice. Not long ago, I was recounting some of the lessons He took me through, and I felt to begin writing about them. I will try to express the struggle through the process to encourage others to keep trying and moving forward in their own walk. Maybe some of this will be confirmation, some of it a bit out there, and for some it may be beyond where you are...but wherever you are on your journey of walking with the Lord, be assured He wants you to hear Him more than you want to, and He is always speaking and directing; we just need to learn and understand all the different ways for us individually...

Thirteen years ago, I encountered the Holy Spirit of God, but prior to that, I walked the Christian life as best as I knew how at the time. I went to church, was involved in church, and gave and served in every area I was able. I would pray from a prayer structure that was very simple and was all I knew. I was always in awe and intimidated by people who really prayed with power, and also, who could pray long prayers. I would try to read the Bible every day, but only every once in a while did I get some encouragement from it. For nineteen years, I lived a Christian life filled with questions and struggles, and was clueless how to truly hear from the Lord. Yes, every once in a while I would feel a type of inspiration and would act on it, but did not recognize it as the Lord's leading.

So, unknown to me, my journey of hearing the Lord's voice began when I began pursuing whether He was real or not. Unfortunately, my life was very full with two children and running a business, and so, I was looking for ways to lessen the demands on my life and church. I spent many hours serving on committees and everything else, and so, if God was not real, then that would free up so much time. I decided I would remove myself from many of the committees to free up time to learn if He was real. I began crying out to Him with all that was within me to show me He was real. I had no idea how to walk through this discovery, but I just knew I needed to do it. I now see that He was drawing me in...

As I turned my focus to discovering Him, I soon became more aware of the possibility that He might be real. I did not know what it would look like or feel like, but I pursued Him in whatever way I could. We took a work and witness team to Australia three weeks after 9/11, and that is when it began. I was the leader of the team, and so, that put me with the responsibility of the money for the team. I had a money bag and the money kept multiplying in the bag. I cannot explain it, but the more I gave out, the more there was in the bag. It was confounding me as I have a financial mind and I document every dime with a receipt, and when all was said and done, I had $750.00 more than what we started with. I had receipts to document every dime of the original, but I had this extra money. To this day, I do not know how He did it, but this was my "burning bush" like Moses experienced. He got my attention.

Also, on that trip He gave me a vision, and so, I walked out what He was showing me to do in the vision for that day, and it was amazing. Again, He was getting my attention in directing my path like I would perceive it happened with people in the Bible. When we returned from the trip, we were sitting in church and I heard the audible voice of God tell me that this was our last Sunday here. I remember looking around wondering who just spoke that loudly during church, but no one around me seemed to have heard it. So, I told my husband what had happened, and after 19 years at the same church, we left to see where He was leading us. We tried a couple churches but when we walked into this one, somehow I knew this was the one. I spent the next 6 months pressing my face into the altar every time it was offered, and I cried out to the Lord to show me He was real. Again, I did not know what I was truly asking for, I just knew there was more, and so, I went after Him. He did not let me down, and soon, one evening I encountered Him. My life was forever changed...

His word was alive like never before, and my prayer life was my life. I have no real words to describe the Holy Spirit change within me. All I knew was He answered my prayers, and I knew, beyond a shadow of a doubt, that He was real. And so, the journey of hearing His voice began...I had longed to be able to hear lots of words from the Lord, and yet, they just seemed to come in one or two word revelations. One night, I was driving home from a Bible study and asking the Lord why I hear just a couple words while others hear and speak so many. What was wrong with me? He began speaking to me this...My child, when you are a child you learn to speak one word at a time and then words connect, and soon sentences, and then paragraphs, and before you know it, conversations happen. It is the same with hearing My voice, it is a process.

He communicated to me through visions, dreams, speaking to me, through His word, and anything and everything around me. One day, as I was getting ready in the morning, He said to me that today we were going to do 'A Thought for the Day'. I had no idea what He was talking about, and so, He showed me in a vision a computer screen with an email ready to be filled in. So, I said, "Okay." At first I just used a quote from a book and sent it out to everyone in my address book. But soon He was expanding the quotes and began dictating messages to me. This would happen at any time day or night, and I would wait for it. When He said it was time to write, I would stop what I was doing, open up the email, and wait for Him to begin speaking. He would tell me word for word, and usually it was about something that was within my day. He used everything in the world around me to speak to me. After I would write, I would read it at least ten times; as it was something I did not know about prior. I was amazed. I began looking for what He could possibly use and anticipated His leading to write. I have to confess that I was not always overjoyed at His timing, as sometimes He would wake me up in the middle of the night and say it was time to write. Or worse yet, I was having a really bad day and had absolutely no desire to write an encouraging email to everyone. I was in process...

Finally, after nine months of writing nearly every day, He showed me a computer screen with the words 'It is finished' on it. So, I sat down at the computer and typed what I saw and sent it out. The messages of this type stopped that day. I had given birth (nine months) to hearing and obeying His voice and learning to look for Him in everything around me, as He will speak to me through everything.

My journey soon transitioned into hearing and obeying His voice at a whole new level. I recall one time that we were planning a vacation to go to two islands in Hawaii over the Christmas and New Years weeks. I felt the Lord leading and telling us to go. Unfortunately, the timeshare places were not in total agreement with our going, but He told me to book the tickets and rental cars and to go. We had gotten a place for the first week, but the second week was not secured. This was way beyond my comfort zone, but we obeyed and went. On Wednesday of the first week, I was calling to find out if they had found us a place to stay yet, as we were leaving on Saturday for Maui and we needed a place to stay. All I kept hearing was that was the busiest week of the year and there was no unit on the entire island available. All the Lord kept telling me was to trust Him, so I did as best I could, considering the circumstances. While we were waiting, we decided to go on a whale-watching boat ride. While we were waiting with all the other people to get on the boat, the Lord spoke to me to get on the right side of the boat. I thought that was a bit odd and did not totally listen. He said it again and told me to tell my family (yes, I was not alone on this journey, which increased the pressure) and so I did. When we finally were able to get on the boat, everyone was on the left side, but we obeyed and got on the right side of the boat. It did not make sense to me, but I felt I heard Him very clearly, so we stood on the right side of the boat by ourselves. As the boat pulled out of the harbor, guess what...a couple whales popped up out of the water right in front of us. Wow God! As I look back now, I think I was in a season of obey/reward and it encouraged me to trust further. Just amazing...

Well, back to where we were going to stay for the second week of our trip...when we got back to our place we were staying, I called again, and nothing. On Thursday morning, I called again, and nothing. I was agonizing over this situation, as I was always the one who had everything planned, and yet, this time I did not. As I look back at all of this now, my husband must have had enormous grace over him from the Lord to just let me walk this out, as it made no sense at all. On Friday morning, (we had a flight out on Saturday morning heading to the other island), the phone rang and they had found a one-bedroom place, so I told him I would let him know because we had asked for a two-bedroom place, and this did not totally fit what we asked for. It was not super peaceful in our timeshare unit at that moment, because I did not have peace about it, so I spent time with the Lord asking Him what He wanted us to do. I kid you not...He said to let it go. I reminded Him of our flight out in the morning and that we would have no place to stay, and He just told me to trust Him.

I came out from this time with the Lord and announced to my family that the Lord said to let it go and to trust Him. This created quite a stirring of emotions and words, and I was not the hero in anyone's eyes. Again, I want to preface all of this with the fact that my family had to have been covered by HUGE grace from God to walk this with me and not just step in and say this is enough. So, I called the gentleman back and told him we were letting the one-bedroom go, and he very kindly let me know that there was absolutely nothing else and I should take it. I said, "Thank you, but we will let it go." I asked him to keep searching for a two-bedroom unit. When I hung up the phone, my family left the room, very upset with me. This had pushed them to the limit. I stood at the kitchen sink doing the dishes, crying out to the Lord. Tears were flowing out everywhere. I felt as if I had just let my family down and they were all upset with me. I kept asking the Lord to please show Himself strong here, and to bring the two-bedroom unit soon. Again, I reminded Him of our flight in the morning and that I was trying to trust Him and believe Him... "please" kept coming out of my mouth through the tears. Ten minutes later, the phone rang, and as I picked up the phone, my family all appeared to hear the conversation. The man on the other end of the phone told me he does not know how it happened, but a two-bedroom unit on Maui just came available, and it would be available tomorrow. I told him we would take it. Wow, that was intense, and amazing, and filled with every extreme emotion I had. He did it. Everything came together and we finished the vacation without changing any flights, and we did not have to sleep on the beach or in our rental car...we had a great week.

This was just the beginning of my learning to hear His voice, it was intense training, but has changed me forever...

CHAPTER 3
It's a Conversation

Whether in the church or not, I feel that everyone at some point in their life struggles with how to communicate with God. How do we talk to the One who knows everything? How do we talk to the One who created everything, including us? Is there a right way or a wrong way? Many approach it with a fear of saying the wrong thing and getting in trouble, possibly like we learned in childhood or other relationships in our past and present. Some are mad at Him and do not want to talk to Him, except maybe to tell Him He is wrong or to yell at Him. We have, most likely, heard messages on prayer or read books on prayer like this one. Depending on whom you listen to or where you are from, you will, and most likely have, gotten differing thoughts on this subject.

Whether it was learned, or you are reacting out of your past, influences your views on talking to God. I, too, have had all of the same struggles. In prayer meetings, I have listened to people pray and thought that is how God wants us to pray because they sounded so wonderful. The enemy wants us to compare our prayers to those of others. He tries either to make us feel inadequate or superior when we do this. Comparison is dangerous and leads us down a path to where we do not pray at all or struggle with it, or we take over the whole prayer meeting.

Prayer is a conversation with God. As in any relationship, communication is vital to its growth. I, personally, have felt that the Lord wants us to talk to Him. I like to stay in communication with Him all day long. I talk to Him when I wake up, while I'm reading His word, over a cup of coffee, while I'm writing in my journal, on my walk, doing the dishes, hanging the laundry on the line, in the car, and even when I'm listening to someone else talk. He is my best friend and I love to talk to Him. I trust Him. I talk to Him when I am upset, sad, hurt, confused, need direction or help, need wisdom and pretty much through any emotional challenge I face. I trust Him.

Over the years, I have found Him to be the safest person to whom I talk. He is a great listener. He knows what is going on better than I ever will. He knows why I am upset, what triggered me, what the other person did or did not do, and He does not run to someone else and tell them my issues. He is safe. I have learned that He is for me and loves me no matter what. I pay attention when He speaks because I know that it is important, and He is going to tell me exactly what I need. He does not put me down or get angry with me. He is always available and always has time for me. I love to talk to Him.

IT'S A CONVERSATION

I love mornings when I hear the Lord ask me to have coffee. I get my coffee, and then I sit and listen to what He has to say. Many times I write it down because it is important. I value His thoughts. I love when He tells me He is with me in a situation because I know He is. We have a relationship. It has been developed over years and hours of conversation. For me, prayer is talking to God and having a conversation. I do not believe that He is concerned about what we say as long as we are trying to talk to Him. Now, do not take that wrong. I am not saying that we get to tell God what to do or not do. I am not saying He is overjoyed if we curse and swear at Him, but I do think He will listen because it is a start of a relationship.

There are days when I wake up and feel very distant from the Lord, and I do fight a bit with trying to talk to Him. On those types of mornings, I purpose to praise and thank Him for what He has done and who He is. While doing that, I am also asking Him what is wrong with me. I search my heart to see if I have un-forgiveness somewhere. I repent and ask Him to forgive me, and I forgive myself. I talk to Him about me, my family, my future…I pray for my family, for others, the world or anything that He brings to mind. I greatly value talking to Him and processing life with Him. He is my Counselor, Friend, Helper, Encourager, Healer, Listener, Advisor, Dad, and I love Him. He loves me. I have come to understand and trust His love for me.

Some days are amazing. I feel Him so close. Prayer and conversation go back and forth, and I never want it to stop. But it is not always that way. What relationship is?

He is the constant in my life. It has developed one day at a time, one conversation at a time, one challenge at a time...He is my peace! I know He is there whether I feel Him or not, I just know He is there. We have history together.

If you are struggling with how in the world to pray...just get a cup of coffee and find your comfortable spot, and have a conversation. Tell Him how you are doing and what you are struggling with. Ask Him to help you and show you what to do. Admit that you have a bad attitude or that you are mad at Him. (If you are mad at Him, you might want to read my book Given to Forgive. It will help you get free of this.)...He can handle it. He already knows it is there, anyway. He is not mad. He will not ignore you; we ignore Him. He will listen, and hope that you, too, will listen to Him. But if you do not, He will patiently wait until you come to Him again. He is patient and kind. Purpose to have a conversation with Him as a friend, get to know Him in His Word, ask Him to break down all of your fears, false perceptions, and inaccurate ideas on prayer, and to teach you how to have a conversation with Him. Then your journey into prayer will begin...enjoy!

CHAPTER 4
Talking to Whom?

When you pray, who do you naturally address? We pray or talk with whom we feel most comfortable. Pay attention next time you pray, is it Our Father, Heavenly Father, Father God, God, Lord, Lord Jesus, Holy Spirit...who? As far as if He, the Three-in-One, is listening or not due to how we address Him, I do not think it matters. But it can be insightful for us personally.

For a very long season, I began a conversation in prayer with Lord. At one point, I heard the Lord ask me to call Him Dad. I was not able to do it. To me, it felt disrespectful to call the God of the Universe, Dad. As I looked at it further, it was difficult because when I tried to call Him Dad, it connected with my earthly father. First of all, I did not want to place how my earthly dad did things on Him. I, also, did not want to disrespect my earthly dad and replace him with God. My earthly father died years ago and he was the only one I called dad. So, this was challenging inside of me. Our fathers are to be protecting us, keep us secure, provide for us and be there for us as safe, strong, and wise. I actually had to work on my heart and mind for several months. I asked the Lord to forgive me for not seeing Him as my Dad, and I forgave myself. I also had to work on forgiving my earthy dad for things that he did. How our earthly father treated us, and how we communicated with him, influences how we see and view our Heavenly Father.

It took me several months to be able to address God as Dad. I did a lot of forgiving of my earthly dad; he was not a Christian, and a lot of repenting and forgiving myself, too. But, once I was able to address Him as Dad, my prayer life took on a whole new perspective. I came to Him as my Dad. I would talk to Him as my Dad. When I found myself in a tough situation, I went to my Dad to talk to Him about it. I remember one time when I said, "Dad, I really need You to be a Dad right here, so please be my Dad and help me with this." When I heard myself say this, I knew I was finally free. I do not always talk to Him as Dad, and many times He is still my Father or Almighty God, but when I need a Dad, He is there, and I feel safe and secure to come to Him as my Dad.

I was, then, taken into a season of addressing the Holy Spirit. I cannot say I talked to Him a lot in this way. The way that we view the Holy Spirit is connected to our relationship with our earthly mother. Think about it, our mothers are to be comforting, good listeners, helpers, counselors, wise, and always there for us. This is who the Holy Spirit is inside of us. Look at John 14:26, "But the Helper, the Holy Spirit whom the Father will send in

My name He will teach you all things, and bring to your remembrance all things that I said to you." This is who He is to us. But if the relationship with our earthly mother was not healthy, then we do not have a healthy view of the Holy Spirit helping us. If we are not able to talk to our earthly mom, then we are going to have difficulty talking to the Holy Spirit. So, I went to work on my heart and mind and forgave my mom, who also was not a Christian, and I asked the Holy Spirit to forgive me, and I forgave myself. This was not a one-time session, but many times, like 70 times 7 times of forgiving to finally feel safe with the Holy Spirit. I have now learned to rely on the Holy Spirit all the time. It is wonderful.

The next area that was addressed was Jesus. Although, I was saying Lord, it was vague and was not really directed to the Father, Jesus, or the Holy Spirit. It was vague on purpose, not that I was totally aware of it, but inside of me was avoiding all three of Them personally. Well, Jesus is connected to our earthly siblings (Proverbs 18:24). The relationship we have with our earthly sibling's sets up how we relate to Jesus. If we had very good relationships, then Jesus is easy to approach. If our relationships were strained, as mine were, then approaching Jesus was not my first choice. My brother and I always fought. This is not actually something that I was aware of, but it was a tendency because of the earthly relationship. I went to work on my heart and mind in this area, too. I forgave my brother and asked the Lord to forgive me, and I forgave myself...yes, 70 times 7, yet again. I soon felt safe to talk to Jesus and call Him by name. It was so very healing.

Whom we address does not matter to Them, but it makes a world of difference to us. They are Three-in-One to completely and fully be there for us in every situation and circumstance. They are not in competition with each other. They do not get jealous of each other. They all work in complete harmony to be fully there for us. It is hard to explain, but I know this from experience now, that I can speak to any One of Them at any time and They meet that deep, secure need in just the way I need it. As I worked on all of these relationships, my trust, confidence, security, hope, faith and prayer life changed significantly. Sometimes I even speak to all three of Them...It was such a healing process on so many levels. To Whom do you talk?

I wanted to add one other thing into this chapter. We have authority when we ask for things in the Name of Jesus. It is as if we come to a closed up area, and the only way we can get through is with the Name of Jesus. We come in His Authority and not ours. He paid the price. He did it. He knows what to do. He is capable of anything. He can do anything. When we come up against a stronghold or demonic spirit or sickness or anything that Jesus came up against, we come in His Authority and He makes the way for us. In John 14:13-14, "And whatever you ask in My name, that I will do, that the Father may be glorified in the Son. If you ask anything in My name, I will do it." I picture it like a movie where a servant needs to speak to a king. The king does not just meet with anyone, but certain people who have authority and access. When we come in the Name of Jesus, it brings access and the enemy has to back down.

TALKING TO WHOM?

So, not only think about how you begin your conversations in prayer, but also how you end them...

CHAPTER 5
What Does He Do?

I read Psalm 139:23, "Search me, O God, and know my heart; try me, and know my anxieties;" and I just stopped. I thought about how many times I have read this verse and others like it, and came into agreement with these words for me. I thought about the songs I have sung asking the Lord, or even telling the Lord, to take my heart, and all of the other songs that are prayers. I thought about the cries of my heart and what I have asked the Lord in those moments. What do we think He is going to do with those prayers? Do we think or pray, thinking He is going to give us a one-time answer? What does He do with our prayers?

Do we pray something one time or agree with something one time, and never think about it again? What does He do with those prayers? Lately, I have realized He thoroughly answers these prayers, and does not complete the answer until the answer is complete in us. Think about that...

Long after we have moved on from some of our prayers, He has not. Look at Zacharias in Luke 1:13, "But the angel said to him, "Do not be afraid, Zacharias, for your prayer is heard, and your wife Elizabeth will bear you a son, and you shall call his name John."" Zacharias is old when he has an angel come and deliver the answer to a prayer that he and his wife prayed many years ago. Think about it, was he still asking in his old age, or had he just moved on from asking? God did not move on. He heard the prayers, and in His own timing, the answer was given.

So, when we look again at the verse from Psalm 139, and we pray that, what do we think the answer is going to look like? Are you currently in a trial? Do you have anxiety or worry? Have you ever in your lifetime come into agreement with this verse above? You might be right in the middle of the answer to your prayer...think about that...

I am thinking there are times we wrestle with and struggle with our own answers to our prayers. Is this verse not asking for the writer to be placed into trials? Do the songs that we sing in church mean more than we realize when we sing? Do we mean them in the moment, but forget after we leave the building? We might need to be a little more mindful of the words we sing and the prayers we pray because He is listening. This gives a little deeper meaning to the words in Proverbs where we read that life and death are in the power of the tongue...

We might need to spend a little time thinking this through and begin thanking Him for the answers to the prayers we prayed that got us into the mess in which we might find ourselves...Maybe He wants us to see what is inside of us so we can get free of it...He thoroughly and completely answers...maybe not in the way we thought it should be answered, but He does hear and answer...I am going to be thankful through it all...

CHAPTER 6
Practical Intercession

I had one of those days. On Tuesday mornings, I had a Women's Bible Study in my home, and one day, no one showed up until an hour later. I was all prepared, sat, and waited. While I waited, the enemy wanted me to get discouraged and upset. I looked at that choice, and instead, chose to pray for all the other leaders of groups who had no one show up. I really pressed into what I felt the enemy was trying to get me to agree with and used it as a guide to pray for the others.

It did not take very long for the enemy to leave me alone, as his plan was not working. I soon felt much better and actually encouraged. I have found that, so many times, we can turn our own struggles and challenges into intercession for others and get out from under the heaviness of our situation.

Another time, I was waiting in a turn lane for the traffic to clear so I could turn. As I sat there, I asked the Lord to please clear the traffic so that I could cross. I heard Him say in response, "What about all of the people behind you?" It caught my attention and I realized my prayers were a bit selfish, and so, I prayed for everyone behind me, and for those who would get into this turn lane for the rest of the day. I was then in a parking lot looking for a space to park, and I was asking the Lord to please open up a space for me. Again I heard Him say, "What about all of the other people driving around looking for a space?" I prayed for them as well. These little interactions with intercession have changed my whole perspective...

So, today, if you are overwhelmed with your financial situation, pray for the other people who are in that situation, too. Use exactly how you are feeling to show you how to pray. This powerful weapon of warfare can be used with every single situation in which you find yourself. Believe me, there are always people who are in the same situations as you. You do not have to know their names; just pray for all the people all over the world who are in your situation. You get your eyes off of yourself, and you are used of God to help others who you may never know.

What are you burdened by? You know how to pray for others. God is so good! God causes all things to work together for the good (Romans 8:28).

CHAPTER 7
Teach Us How to Pray

More people than we know struggle to pray. They struggle to find the time, the place, and even how to do it. I know, I was one of those who, for years, struggled to pray, and I would never have admitted that to anyone. My personal prayer life was shallow. I had a little prayer list and I broke it down to each day of the week, and would say a brief prayer for each item and forget about it for the rest of the day. I did not spend hours in prayer. I did not know how to spend time with the Lord, and I ignored the fact most of the time, feeling my acts of service to the church count as time spent with Him. I would try to tithe 10% of my time as I did my money. Some weeks I did really well and others fell short. I was not trying to spend time out of desire, but out of obligation.

Since my private prayer life was quite limited, my public prayer life also was limited. I would very seldom pray out loud, and even more seldom pray out loud for another person. I never wanted to be called on to pray in a group; you know how you can look down or away not to make eye contact with the person delegating the closing or opening times of meetings. That was me. I cannot say I wanted a prayer life or even wanted to learn. I did not really know what I did not know...

I know that I am not alone in this. So, how does this change? For me, it was the Holy Spirit. I finally came to a place in my life where I submitted control to Him, and I encountered the Holy Spirit. My prayer life changed and deepened. I enjoyed praying, and praying for others, too. It can happen; do not lose heart. I was a strong-willed, independent, hard-hearted woman. I finally had enough and submitted to Him being Lord of my life. Yes, nineteen years prior, I accepted Jesus into my heart, but that was about as far as I let Him in. I did not trust anyone by that point in my life. So, if it can happen to me, it can happen to you. Please keep reading...

So, how do we pray, anyway? Well, the disciples realized they did not know how to pray in Luke 11:1, "Now it came to pass, as He was praying in a certain place, when He ceased, that one of His disciples said to Him, "Lord, teach us to pray, as John also taught his disciples."" Look at that for a moment. The disciples have already been sent out twice, once with 12 and then with 72. They experienced miracles, and even came back and told Jesus about it in Luke 10:17-20. This tells us that Jesus did not teach them how to pray. Isn't that odd? Maybe it appears that way, but maybe not. I think they were asking Jesus for more of what He had. They saw Him when He came down off the mountains, when He returned from certain places, the secluded places...they watched Him and listened to Him, and they knew there was something very different about Jesus. They determined it was prayer, so they asked Him to teach them how to pray.

After this question, we find the well-known "Lord's Prayer". Much of the world knows this prayer. It is recited all the time. But His intention wasn't for it just to be recited, but to use it as a model or guide. Open up your Bible to Luke chapter 11, I will wait (smile)... The first two lines that Jesus tells them, (Our Father in heaven, hallowed be Your name) is showing honor, respect, and reverence to the Father. This comes when we humble ourselves, and I put thanksgiving in here as well. The next two lines (Your kingdom come. Your will be done on earth as it is in heaven.) are submission and bowing down. We are bowing down our will. I will tell you, if these first four lines do not come into place with our submitting to Almighty God knowing better than we do, we might as well stop praying, because everything after that is going to be self-centered and focused on us (did I say that out loud? Yep). So, the first four lines are guidelines for how we draw near to Him in honor, respect, and reverence to the One who knows us so well. We honor Him by giving Him our undivided attention at this moment. We respect Him by listening to Him and valuing what He has to say to us, whether He is directly speaking to us or through His Word. We show reverence by gratitude, acknowledging who He is and His hand in our life. The first two lines adjust our attitude, because as He draws near, we become aware of our junk. So, we acknowledge He is God and we are not by our words, attitudes, posture, thoughts, and actions.

As we humble ourselves in the site of the Lord, He will lift us up (James 4:10). In the world, we would be rejected, and He lifts us up. At the beginning, it is difficult to trust this. We know we have sinned and made poor choices, and so, we are afraid. But, keep going with me on this, it is not that difficult and does not have to take a long time. Verse 3, "Give us day by day our daily bread" is in regards to provision. Provision is physical, Spiritual, mental, and emotional. Think about it, allow the beginning of honoring, respecting and gratitude to even come through this area in regards to His complete provision for you.

Verse 4, "And forgive us our sins, for we also forgive everyone who is indebted to us" is forgiveness. If you have not read my book, "Given to Forgive", I would encourage you to do so to gain understanding of forgiveness, and why this line is important in His teaching. In this area of prayer, we forgive others, God, and ourselves. With unforgiveness in our hearts, we limit our communication with God. If we are angry at God and need to forgive Him, then we are certainly not going to want to talk to Him or listen to Him. This verse is critical to our prayer life and relationship with the Father, the Son, and the Holy Spirit.

The next line, "And do not lead us into temptation, but deliver us from the evil one" is direction and protection which we need from Him. Be specific; admit that you need His help and direction. Talk to Him as a child speaking to their Dad.

We need to go to Matthew 6 to get the closing, "For Yours is the kingdom and the power and the glory forever. Amen." Again, we are closing with honor, respect, reverence, and acknowledgment. This is how He taught them to pray. It starts with our individual relationship with Him. Our confidence in praying for other people and praying aloud in groups begins in private. When I pray for other people, I'm talking to Him on their behalf. I am not talking to them. They just get to overhear the conversation, like we do in John 17, when Jesus is praying for Himself, His disciples, and for the generations in the future.

Is this how I always pray? Absolutely not, but when I wake up in the morning and I cannot figure out how to pray, I step into this. Is this the only way to pray? No, it is a helpful guide to get you started. It is not the only way, but it is a way. We cannot discount what Jesus said. Remember He is the way, the truth and the life for each of us. If you look at the bigger picture of this prayer, you will see a lifestyle of living a life submitted to God.

Our confidence in prayer comes from studying Jesus, talking to Him, spending time with Him, listening, worshiping, and learning. The more we understand and know Him, the more we trust Him and trust that He hears us and will help the person in front of us.

Let me let you in on a secret; He wants to talk to you. He wants you to get to know Him and trust Him. He loves you like none other. Spend time in Luke 11 and John 17, study the words that Jesus spoke and prayed, and then read the Gospels and discover how He walked out what He taught. He came to be our example, learn from Him...

CHAPTER 8
Jesus Prays

Throughout the Gospels we read that Jesus prayed. He went up on the mountain, early in the morning and prayed. We witness Him praying for the sick, the dead, the lame, the deaf, the leapers, the mute, the demon possessed, and in the garden prior to His arrest. But most of those prayers are not recorded as very long. We do not get to over hear His conversations with the Father up on the mountain, or the conversation with Moses and Elijah at the transfiguration (Matthew 17:1-13), but we know it happened.

The Gospel of John is the only Gospel that records a long prayer of Jesus before being arrested. This is found in John chapter 17; take some time and read it. It is one of my favorite chapters in the Bible. We get to overhear a conversation between Jesus and His Father. It is not here by accident and is intentional for us today. I have spent a lot of time reading this chapter over and over and there is much to learn from it.

Earlier in His ministry, His disciples asked Him to teach them how to pray in Luke chapter 11 (a chapter prior, "Teach Us How to Pray"), but this chapter is Jesus taking the Lord's Prayer to a whole new level. The subtitles in my Bible break it down into three sections, "Jesus Prays for Himself", "Jesus Prays for His Disciples", and "Jesus Prays for All Believers". I, too, will write into these three sections to simplify what I learned.

Jesus prays for Himself in verses 1-5. We need to remember that He knows what is coming. Everything He came to do is getting ready to close out and be finished. Every word He is speaking is important. Just as we can read the whole story and know what is going to happen to Him, He knows it, too. He knows it is not going to be easy and it is going to be messy. This is the Jesus who is the same yesterday, today, and forever (Hebrews 13:8) speaking. This is the Jesus who gives us the strength to do all things (Philippians 4:13) speaking. This is the Jesus who came to be an example to us (1 Peter 2:21-24), speaking. Are we listening? As He prays for Himself, we can learn how to pray for ourselves. Do we ever ask God to glorify us, that we may glorify God? Do we think this way? Do we live our lives purposing to please and honor Him? This changed how I pray. Listen to Him speaking. Be grateful and praise Him for what He did for us.

Listen to Him in verse 4, "I have glorified You on the earth. I have finished the work which You have given Me to do." Do we think this way? Do we think about the work that He has given us to do? This turned into a prayer for me. Help me, God, to glorify You on this earth and to finish the work that You have given me to do.

This changes how I view my day. Within each day that I live and breathe there is a purpose for me, within the people that I cross paths with, the challenges that I face, the issues that come up, the words I speak and write, and the prayers I pray...there is purpose. I was not just dropped here to try to exist. I am not here by accident. I want to finish the work within each day that He has given me to do. So, this is my prayer. We are not Jesus, but we are witnesses of Him. He is living inside of us and is willing and able to help us with our purpose; we need to choose it. If Jesus needed to pray this, then I do, too.

Jesus, then, prays for His disciples, verses 6-19. These are the men He has been teaching and training. These are the men who have been walking with Him privately and publically. God called these men to be with Him. We, also, have people around us who we are teaching and training. As a mother, I have children who are within my influence. What am I doing with them for their future? What am I modeling to them with my actions, words, and choices in my daily life with them? This prayer of Jesus became deeply personal to me as I looked at the people who are around me. I began to realize that they are intentionally there, and I am intentionally in their lives. From my children, to my husband and family, to neighbors, people I speak to, friends and so many more; this prayer of Jesus for His disciples became my prayer for the people He has given me.

Jesus, then, prays for all believers, verses 20-26. He is praying for the people, like you and me, in the future. This prayer is for us. I read it carefully and slowly, listening to how He was praying for me (and you). He is thinking about you and me while praying this. I, then, took this as my own prayer for future generations that will come after me. What I give to the people He has given me, will be given to others I will never see or to whom I will never speak. It brings greater value to every moment that I am living in now. The words that I write and speak now have an influence on the future. My books are how I hand my faith to future generations. My messages that are recorded are handing my faith to future generations. I want to leave notes for them in my journals. I want to think about them now, as Jesus did, so that I can leave them a part of my faith. This is what Jesus is doing. It became a part of me as I came into agreement with this prayer for me and allowed it to become my prayer for my future generations.

These last words and prayers of Jesus are of significant value for us today. Take some time and allow them to become part of your thinking and reasoning. Allow purpose to rise up inside of you. Read it many times and agree with it. Embrace His words for you and your family and future generations. This has changed my thinking and I pray it changes yours as well...

CHAPTER 9
Prayer That Changes Me

Over the years, I have learned that some days it is easy to pray and some days I have to figure out how to pray. I have had days where I could not figure out what to pray about or how to even begin to pray. I am just flat and feeling nothing. I do not like those days at all, and I know they can be dangerous to my relationship with God if I do not press through it. Why does this happen? I am not always sure; sometimes I have a lot going on in my life and I have let that influence my thoughts more than it should, or other times I have un-forgiveness blocking me, or sometimes it is just warfare and what is happening around me. Whatever it is, I purpose to press through it. One way I have discovered to press through is to use what is around me and pray into it. I use it as a pattern or guide. I have found the body the Lord gave us is a great place to start. One morning I began praying like this (you can come into agreement with it for yourself, too)...

Lord Jesus, thank You for me! I thank You for the color of my hair, the sound of my voice, the color of my skin. I thank You for the color of my eyes, the way that I look, the shape of my body, and my health. I thank You for my mind and how You made it to think and process. Thank You that my mind can reason and understand. Thank You that my mind is keeping my body alive and functioning. I thank You for renewing my mind. Forgive me for the thoughts that are not of You and please help me to have thoughts that please, honor and glorify You. Thank You that I have the mind of Christ and with the mind of Christ I can do all things. Thank You for my eyes and for giving me eyes to see. Thank You that my eyes get to enjoy the amazing world that You have placed around me. Thank You for my ears and their ability to hear You and Your voice and direction, to hear and enjoy music and the sounds of the world You created. Thank You for my mouth and my voice. Thank You that my mouth has influence and help me to recognize the significant influence that it has in the world around me. Thank You for the ability to eat through my mouth. Thank You for my teeth, my tongue, my saliva, my taste buds, and my ability to chew and swallow. I thank You for my nose, the shape of it, that it can smell and enjoy the incredible fragrances that You have placed on this earth for us to enjoy. Thank You for the bone structure of my face. Thank You for my eyelashes, eyebrows, and for my healthy skin. I thank You for my throat and esophagus, and neck. I thank You for my thyroid, and spinal cord. I thank You for my endorphins, and nervous system. I thank You for my joints and ligaments. I thank You for my shoulders, elbows, and wrists. I thank You for my hands and fingers and joints that can touch, hold, and wear jewelry such as my wedding ring. Thank You for what my hands allow me to do in the world around me...to write and communicate, to turn the pages of Your Word, to drive a car, to hold my coffee, to pet my dogs, to hold my children's and husband's hands, to touch someone and let them know they are not alone. Thank You that my hands can work and praise You! Thank You for my arms that can praise, hug, hold, embrace, carry, lift, catch, and work. Wow, thank You for every single aspect that goes into my arms and hands... the bones, the tendons and ligaments, the veins that run through them. Wow, Your creativity inside of me and how I work is amazing, thank You.

Lord Jesus, I thank You for my heart, lungs, and rib cage. I thank You for my back and spinal cord. I thank You for my stomach, pancreas, kidneys, gallbladder, bladder, stomach, and liver, intestines small and large. I thank you for my reproductive system (ladies go into detail here, I'm not because men will be reading this). I would encourage you to go into great detail thanking Him for every part of you and what He made you to be able to do and create inside of you. Men, thank Him for who He made you to be. Lord Jesus, I thank You for my hips, legs, knees, bones, ankles, and feet and toes. I thank You that I am able to walk, run, jump, kneel, and bend. I thank You for my muscles and everything else that works together to give me this ability. I thank You for balance in my body. I thank You for my blood cells red and white. I thank You for how detailed You are with me. I am in awe of You and I thank You for me. Forgive me for the times that I have not appreciated or cared for the body that You have given me. Help me to take better care of it, to desire the food necessary, to exercise to keep it strong, and to appreciate it. Please restore every part of my body back to its original function and please touch me and bring total health to my body. Thank You Jesus, thank You! Amen!!

This changes me. This opens up prayer every time. I discovered there are some parts of me I was challenged to be thankful for; I asked the Lord to forgive me and I needed to forgive myself, too. There were some areas that I needed to forgive God, not that He had done anything wrong, but I thought He did. We can be very mentally and physically destructive to our own bodies. Being thankful for who He created us to be brings health and healing. Go into even more detail than I have here... this is just a start; you take it from here.

I realized as I was writing this, that other things could rise up with a mixed audience. I pray your minds will remain pure and that you will pray this for yourself, and not fantasize about someone else or even me. Do not allow the enemy to bring bad through this. I am not leaving it out because there are too many people this will help. I pray protection over this chapter in the name of Jesus!!

CHAPTER 10
Awareness Awakened

Several years back, I attended a church that had an offering reading and the whole church would say it aloud. I remember feeling empowered as we would read it week after week. Maybe your church does this and maybe it does not, but there is something about it. It is as if my focus is being shifted and my hope is being placed in a faithful, unfailing God who cares about me and loves me. I looked forward to it.

After we quit attending that church, I would still remember that reading. I began saying it each day over my home. At the time, we were in a financially challenged place, so I needed some way to build up my faith and trust. I was shifting my focus from my lack, to the One who can actually make a difference. I felt empowered as I spoke it. I would pray it on my walks. I, then, felt the Lord expanding it, and I began praying it over my husband and I, our daughter and her husband, our son, our future grandchildren and great grandchildren and generations I will never meet. This changed the whole prayer for me. I knew these prayers were making a difference for the future of all of us. I felt like I was making road ways in the wilderness for our family.

As I continued on this journey each day, I began noticing answers to this prayer...I know, you are curious about the prayer...here it is...

OFFERING OF THANKS #1
(Bethel Church)
As we receive today's offering we are believing the Lord for:
Jobs and better jobs,
Raises and bonuses
Benefits, sales and commissions
Favorable settlements
Estates and inheritances
Interests and income
Rebates and returns
Checks in the mail
Gifts and surprises
Finding money
Debts paid off
Expenses decrease
Blessing and increase
Thank You, Lord, for meeting all of my financial needs that I may have more than enough to give into the Kingdom of God and promote the Gospel of Jesus Christ. Hallelujah!!!!!!

Soon, my husband got a job and benefits, sales and commissions. We got a favorable settlement on a situation, my inheritance from my dad began opening up; pretty much every one of these items I recognized as happening. I noticed it for the rest of our family, too. That offertory prayer was making a huge difference. I was proclaiming my belief in God to take care of us.

These areas could have been happening all along, but because I was praying and believing for them, I recognized when they happened. Small little moments when I would get a rebate check in the mail, or find money on the ground, or would go to the store and it was buy one and get one free of exactly what I went in the store to get, or I would get a notice in the mail to refinance our home with no costs and it lowered our payments...the list is endless. As I prayed, my awareness of the Hand of God on our life and His provision opened up. My faith grew. My trust increased. My hope in God was stronger than ever. Yes, He was providing, but I was growing at the same time.

I soon modified the prayers and added things. I personalized them. It is not a formula, but it is taking our faith and impossible situations and placing them in the Hand of God and watching Him take care of us. It has made me so much more thankful because I recognize Him involved in the day in and day out situations and challenges of my day.

I pray this will encourage you to believe the Lord for these areas for your family and future generations... Look at this prayer generationally, I'm praying for jobs for generations I will never meet...everything in this prayer is going ahead of generations coming. If that is not empowering, then I do not know what is.

I wrote this in the front of my journals. I printed it out and carried it with me until I knew it by heart. I wanted always to be aware of the Lord's provision so I could thank Him. It sure got my eyes off of my problems...may this change your recognition...

CHAPTER 11
Praying for Others

When we are given to prayer, we will definitely be faced with the area of praying for other people. This can be intimidating at the beginning. Whether we are given to praying or not, as Christians we will be in settings or situations where we are called on to pray for others. What are our fears? Think about your own, maybe even write them down. I, recently, asked a group of students what they were afraid of when praying for others. The concerns seemed to be: saying the wrong thing, praying prayers that were ineffective, not having the right words, not having anything to pray, and just not knowing how to pray for their needs. Are any of these how you feel?

I wanted to include a chapter to help others get out from under some of the lies that the enemy tells us to keep us from praying for others. This is not all there is to praying for other people, but it is a good start.

First of all, the purpose of praying for another person is for them to encounter Jesus...whether it is one on one, in private or public, in a group, or even over the phone, our prayers have the potential to set up a meeting between them and Jesus. The enemy wants it to be about us and our words, but when we are praying for another person, it is not about us, but them and Jesus. Remember, we are not able to heal them, Jesus is. We are not able to change them, Jesus is. We are not able to fully understand what is actually going on with them, Jesus is. It is not about us, it is about Jesus. We get out of the way and allow Jesus to encounter them. Think about it, when they encounter Jesus everything changes for them...

When praying on a prayer team up front at church, remember the person who stands before you needs your help. If they knew how to pray for the situation they are in, they would not be in front of you. They are not there to evaluate how you pray or how eloquent you put your words together. They need help and need Jesus to help them. Also, keep in mind that they are not in front of you by accident. Jesus wants to touch them through you in that moment. This is a Divine appointment and you are part of it. When He sets it up, He is planning on showing up...just get out of the way and do not allow the enemy to make it about you.

I, personally, do not want to know a lot of information about what is going on with the person; I trust that Jesus already does. Many times people think they need to tell us everything, and we can be listening to them for a long time, and if we are not careful, we can be completely consumed in their issue and not know how to pray for it when they are finished. If they start out talking, just gently place your hand on their shoulder and let them know that Jesus already knows what is going on, so let's talk to Him about it to see what He wants to do about it. Then, we wait on Jesus to show us how to pray. At the beginning this can be quite scary, but do it anyway. When we pray for someone without them telling us what is going on, and we pray how Jesus wants us to pray, they, then, know that Jesus is listening and cares for them. Their faith grows and so does ours. If we allow them to tell us everything that is wrong with them, we, then, are chasing the symptoms and not the solution. They do not know this, but we do, so just kindly stop all of their explanation as I already mentioned...

There are times when I am not sure exactly how to begin praying, so I wait in silence, and I close my eyes not to be distracted by anything going on around us. I pay attention to how I am feeling. If I was fine before the person stood in front of me and now I have a headache or backache or pain anywhere in my body, I pray into that. If I am seeing a picture in my mind, I follow the picture and pray into it. If I am feeling oppressed, then I pray into that. I pay attention to what is happening inside of me and pray; when it lifts from me, I know it lifts from them. If none of the above happens, then I begin thanking Jesus for who He is to them and for them. I ask Jesus to cover them with His love and peace and hope. I have found that after this, I can see how to pray.

When I do come up against challenging situations with people, I will choose to pray in tongues, not loud, but I definitely will pray in the Spirit until I know how to approach the situation and pray effectively. Not everyone has this option, but those who do, will definitely find this helpful. This is different from speaking in tongues in front of a church and waiting for an interpretation. This is prayer, and when I do not know how to pray, I choose this...

Deliverance...I have been through all of the training and have experienced, more than I care to again, situations with people having significant trouble with controlling what is happening inside of them. I have done all of the binding and loosing and clapping and shouting, and have found that most of the time, I am trying to do things that I'm not really sure will work, but I was taught them so I use them, and all the time, inside I feel completely unqualified to be in front of the person. I always felt this way until I began experiencing forgiveness and the power it has. I, also, have a clear understanding of the power of un-forgiveness and what it can do. Now, when I encounter a person being influenced by something negative, I begin asking questions. Are they angry with God? (Read my Given to Forgive book to gain more understanding about forgiveness, if you have not already.) Un-forgiveness opens doors to the enemy to gain access to twist a person's thinking and reasoning. In many cases, they need to forgive God, forgive themselves, and forgive others or organizations, and even all of the above. I work with them to begin forgiving. I am quiet and gentle. As they forgive, the stronghold no longer has a place to hold on to and it leaves. If it has been there for a long time, the person will experience weakness and exhaustion; this is normal. The un-forgiveness has been their source of strength, and it was just removed. Assure them that this unusual feeling is normal, and pray for peace and the filling of the Holy Spirit. It is amazing to experience the sudden change that occurs when they forgive. It is dignified, safe, freeing, powerful, effective and amazing. I do not have to shout, clap, bind or loose…I just help them to forgive…(This process does not work 100% of the time, but it is effective for many situations.)

I would encourage you to study the life of Jesus in the Gospels and to study His word. He left us an example. He showed us what is possible. He, then, is able to recall a Scripture or situation from His word to show us how to pray. So many times He will remind me of a verse or story in His word, and I pray it into the person before me. He uses everything to help us pray. He knows what we know and do not know, and He knows how to communicate with us while we are praying; we just need to pay attention to Him while praying. This is why the enemy tries so hard to get us to think it is about us, then our eyes get off of Jesus, the Solution.

If you are in public and you feel led to pray for someone, ask them if you may pray for them right there. If they say no, then respect that, and let them know you will be praying for them, and then make sure that you do. If they say yes, pray.

When we partner with the Holy Spirit while praying, the time is wonderful, and I, personally, experience times where I get as much out of it as the person I am praying for. But when the Holy Spirit is finished praying, we need to stop praying, too…it is not about the length of the prayer, but what He wants us to pray…

Remember the authority that you have by praying and asking in the Name of Jesus. This gives you authority to ask. Think of a King. Not everyone has access to speak to him unless that person has been given authority to speak. When we pray in the Name of Jesus Christ, this gives us the authority to ask and speak. I like to picture myself coming before the Father and asking in the Name of Jesus for something; it gives me permission to ask. Close your prayers with His Authority...

Here are a couple practical things to remember when praying for another person...

1. Ask them their name and tell them yours.
2. Ask them if you may place your hand on them (respect their answer).
3. Use breath mints and deodorant.
4. Not cool to blow on them.
5. Better not to pray loudly in tongues.
6. Not cool to push them.
7. Inappropriate body contact is not a good idea.
8. Do not draw attention to yourself.
9. Pray with your eyes open.
10. Never pray alone with someone of the opposite sex; the prayee may have been abused or may have emotional ties.
11. Make sure you treat the person you are praying for with respect.

12. Anything prayed for is to be held in confidence, unless permission has been granted to share (or you think leadership needs to know because someone is in danger.)
13. Do not give a lot of advice.
14. Do give a lot of love and acceptance.

Remember:

- People are coming forward for prayer because they need help...
- Praying for another person is not about us, but who we are talking to on behalf of the other person.
- The enemy loves to try to get us to think it is about us----evoking fear---only God can do something...

CHAPTER 12
Parents

Proverbs 22:6, "Train up a child in the way he should go, and when he is old he will not depart from it." There are very few Christians who do not know this verse. Most parents who have grown children are depending on the truth of this verse. But what really is the truth of this verse? I am sorry in advance if this hits too close to home, but it is hitting mine, too...

Do we really realize what we have trained our children to do? Think about it...yes, we teach them to go to church by going to church. But when they get in the car with us and we start complaining about this and that in regards to the service, or what people were wearing, or gossiping about this person and that person...what are we really training them to do? When someone wrongs us and we do not forgive them, and we talk about them behind their back on the phone and we think our kids are in the other room distracted by a television show... what are we really training them to do? When they are playing at the park and they look over at us and we are on the phone, what are we really training them to do? When we travel in the car and put them in front of a movie instead of engaging them in conversation…what are we really training them to do? The things we do…the things we say and do not say…the choices we make with our actions and words are actually training them in the way they should go, whether we are aware of it or not.

Of course, we want them to catch all of the good things we do, but unfortunately, they catch the bad, too. They catch the prejudices, the hypocrisy, the language we use, the anger, the attitudes, the un-forgiveness, the likes and dislikes we have. If our focus is on money and things, theirs, most likely, will be as well. We think it has no effect, but it does, believe me, I see it in my grown children all the time. For those of us with grown children, there is hope, but it starts with us changing first. Maybe we need to go to them and say we are sorry. Maybe we need to tell them how wrong we were. Maybe we need to forgive ourselves and ask God to forgive us and help us to change. Maybe we need to let up on them for the choices they are making, and realize when we were their age, we did the same thing. For me, I have spent a lot of time with the Lord, asking Him how to fix it, and asking Him to forgive me for the poor things I trained them to do…

Part of the redemption of this is this chapter…I want to give to young parents wisdom as I look back. Little things I could have done differently that could have made a significant return for small effort. I want to share some ideas to incorporate into your everyday life for different ages of your children...

Parents of young children, the demands on your time can feel never ending; you are either changing diapers, feeding babies and kids, doing laundry, picking up toys, fixing meals, working a job, comforting hurts, bathing kids, or hundreds of other things, many times all at the same time. If we are not mindful, God is not easily brought into this equation of life. We try, but sometimes it is at the end of the day when the kids are in bed, the dishes are done, the house is back in order, the bills are paid, and it is 10:00 P.M. ... we are exhausted and find it difficult to open our Bible or have a conversation with God other than "HELP".

Try incorporating God into the day with playing worship music, or praying over the clothes you are folding, or teaching your little ones how to have a quiet time with God...depending on the age determines the length of time. Quiet time is established as we are quiet and sit and look at a book, or pray, or listen for God. Parents, please do not be tempted to catch up on Facebook or emails or phone calls during this time, otherwise, guess what you are teaching them...Buy a special seat for them and you. Parents, you get some time with the Lord while this is being taught. After your quiet time, talk to them about what God showed you, and ask what God showed them. Teach them how to hear from God and recognize Him in the world around them. Let them hear you praying, let them see you praying, let them see you reading your Bible...let them see and hear you forgiving and loving others. It starts with small things. If you use time out when your children are having poor behavior, then put yourself in time out when you have poor behavior. When your child is in time out, let them hear you praying for them, not on the phone talking to someone. When you are in time out, ask them to be praying for you. This trains them up in so many things, including taking responsibility for their poor choices when they are grown up. Talk about God, include Him in the day, and look for every opportunity to see Him. Proverbs 22:6, "Train up a child in the way he should go, and when he is old he will not depart from it." Yes, it takes some effort, but what you are sowing into their daily lives is rich and lasting...

As your children get older, modify these things above. Teach them how to be thankful and recognize answers to prayer. When our children were teenagers and we were living by faith in New Zealand, the Lord told me to allow my children to hear and understand the struggle, and to pray with us to see His hand work on our behalf. I realized that if we keep the struggle to ourselves and pray to ourselves and God answers us, they missed the process. Then, when they run into difficulties, they will struggle, because they will remember the testimonies, but will wonder what they did wrong when it just did not happen.

Make it a priority to pray for your children every day. It is an all-out war for your children's hearts and minds. Pray that they will be men or women of truth, and that they will get caught in every lie they tell so they do not get good at it. (I let my children know that I was praying that way, when they were tempted to lie. One time my son came in and was sitting with me, and all of a sudden I heard him say, "Alright, I lied." He would then proceed to tell me about it. Inside I knew it was my prayers that God was answering.) Pray for their future spouse, too, as they are going through the same things. Pray that their heart and mind will remain pure, and you do your part in helping with that in what you watch, look at, listen to, and do. Pray for their protection, their decision making, their health, and the choices which they will face. Begin when they are young and clear paths for them in the future. They are going to have to learn lessons, but pray they submit to them the first time. Pray for their heart always to remain sensitive to the leading of the Holy Spirit. Pray you will be a good example. Repent when you know you have not been the example you feel you should be and forgive yourself. Prayer is your greatest weapon for your child's future. Do not allow yourself to get too tired to pray for them. Pray that He will bring truth to the lies they believe and are being told by others outside of your home. Be given to pray for your children, they need it.

Everything about your life, every second, has the potential to train up your child in the way they should go, and believe me, the good and the bad; they will not depart from it when they are old. If they witness and experience you going to church, but don't witness it in your everyday life the other six days of the week, then that is what you are teaching them about church, and they will, most likely, depart from going to church when they are old, not always, but the potential is there. Recognize your responsibility as the parent, and keep

God in the moments any way you can. I know this is not easy, but it is necessary with the rapid changing world that we live in that is filled with distractions.

Proverbs 22:6, "Train up a child in the way he should go, and when he is old he will not depart from it." May He open your eyes to ideas beyond mine...Save our children, oh God!!

CHAPTER 13
Hindrances to Prayer

I did not know this was going to be a chapter in this book. It seems obvious to me now, but I did not see it. Over the last few months, I have been struggling to get into deep prayer times with the Lord, and even my desire to spend more time with the Lord was fading. I kept asking the Lord why? What is wrong with me? What am I fighting against? What is happening? Although, I felt He was on what was happening, I did not like it.

Years ago, I watched a lot of television. I worked many hours in our business and when the kids were finally in bed at the end of the day, I would sit and watch television to get my mind to shut down from the issues of the day. But over thirteen years ago, we shut off cable to our home because it was just not what we wanted to spend money on, and we did not want it to be our focus. Little by little, over the last few months, I would discover a television show on Netflix's or Hulu. I realized I was falling into the same pattern I was in years ago. There was nothing wrong with the televisions shows I was watching, but I did not like how they were inside of my head. The stories and characters of these shows were in my thoughts, even when the television was off. When I would be praying, they would pop in there. I would sit down to watch one show in the evening and soon it was three. The hook of the story and the hanging ending of the one would get me to watch another. I did not want to do it, but it was happening.

I kept asking Him why? I would repent and ask Him to forgive me, and I would forgive myself, and ask Him to take away the desire and to remove these make-believe stories in my head. This morning, I had had it and I wanted it to stop. That time could I have been spent with Him. That time could have been growing my faith. I was not happy with my perceived lack of discipline. And then, He showed me this chapter, and I realized I had been living through the areas where our prayer life and time with God get hindered. Wow, that was quite a revelation.

Friends, the enemy is subtle with stealing our time away from prayer or time with the Lord. When I say time with the Lord, to me, it is sitting and talking with Him. It is listening to worship music and coming into agreement with it in praising and worshipping God. It is sitting and listening to what He has to say, or reading His word, or writing in my journal, or going for a walk and talking with Him. It is being still before Him. It is choosing Him over the things of this world, because I know one moment with Him is better than thousands in the world. I know one word from Him can change my entire perspective of a situation. I know He knows what is best for me all the time.

I knew the television was becoming a god, but it was hard to stop, even when I knew what I was giving up. Television is effortless, and you do not have to think or do anything. This is exactly what the enemy wants. If he can get us to switch off, he can begin influencing us in ways we are not fully aware. He will tell us lies like, "It does not hurt anything, you deserve this, you are mature enough to watch this, everyone else does this…" Think about it, what is he saying to you? The enemy knows how beneficial our time with the Lord can be, and he works hard at distracting us. Maybe it is not television for you…what about Facebook? Do you catch yourself just scrolling through that news feed only to look up and an hour has passed by? What about sleep? Is sleep more important than prayer? This one is a touchy subject, but pay attention to what is going through your head just reading that…Do you get up in the morning and spend a little time before everyone wakes up, or do you sleep till the last second you can, and then everyone is awake and the demands of life are in full force? The enemy convinces us we need that sleep, but the Lord can strengthen and refresh us in that time with Him. He made us and knows exactly how we work and function. What do we think He means in Matthew 11:28-30, "Come to Me, all you who labor and are heavy laden, and I will give you rest. Take My yoke upon you and learn from Me, for I am gentle and lowly in heart, and you will find rest for your souls. For My yoke is easy and My burden is light." He can give you rest while you are awake. See the lie the enemy is using to get us to make sleep more important, a god, than our time praying and spending time in His word and with Him?

What about that smart phone you have with you 24/7? Those little sounds it makes and we pick it up within moments as if we must see what it is saying. The phone calls, text messages, private messages (especially the ones where it is a group private message and everyone keeps responding and the phone keeps making noises), emails, our calendars...let's face it, all of life can be a distraction from our time in prayer and with Him if we allow it to be. Did you know you can actually control the distractions? I discovered I can turn my phone to silent and turn it face down. It is silent right now as I am writing. I do not want any other gods before Him. Take a look at what takes your time. How can you begin to make changes? How can you discover the rest He wants to give you that is unlike anything the world has to offer? Repent if any of this fits your present condition of life, tell the Lord you are sorry and ask Him to forgive you for making something of this world more important than He, and then forgive yourself. Ask Him to renew your mind and show you how to gain more time with Him. I am up early in the morning before the world starts waking, because I have made Him a priority in my life. I turn off my phone and trust life can wait. I have to fight for the time, but it is so worth the fight.

He gives us insight that changes everything. He brings truth to the lies we believe. He changes relationships, He listens, He has time for us, and He cares more about us than anyone in this entire world. He is worth the fight back. If your prayer life is not very strong, or as strong as you would like it to be, take a look at your choices and see if you can make some changes. Does the television interrupt your thoughts even when it is not on? Can you go an hour without Facebook or your phone? Can you get up a little earlier in the morning and go to bed a little earlier? Ask the Lord how you can change what you do to have more time with Him...It is personal between you and Him. Draw near to Him and He will definitely draw near to you and change everything...

CHAPTER 14
Prayers of Faith or Fear

For the last eleven years, I have been struggling with trusting the Lord with our finances. It was easy to trust Him with our finances when we had our business and we were making a lot of money, but after that, everything changed. In all of my books you will see pieces of this process of trusting Him and His provision. I have been struggling with how to do that. How do I trust Him when the number in the check book is low? I have tried not focusing on it. I have tried ignoring it. I have prayed repeatedly to the Lord to please help me with this. I felt stuck. I felt that money was an idol, but could not figure out how to get free of it. I repented and forgave myself, but still it would show up.

At one point, I realized I thought I could do a better job than God in providing for our family, because I had believed that the success of our business was because of me. I repented and asked the Lord to forgive me and I forgave myself. As time has gone on, the struggle to fully trust Him to provide regardless of what the number was in the checkbook still remained. There were other areas that started pulling on me in regards to ministry, too. I have not been able to figure out how to get free of it, and did not know why it still had a hold of me. I have been crying out to the Lord for many months about this...

A couple weeks ago, my son's car got hit in a parking lot, and the person did not leave any information and take responsibility. Their mistake cost us. I was upset with the Lord as to why it happened. Why didn't He protect our finances? We now had to pay the deductible and that was not budgeted for. Other situations also happened where unexpected expenses arose. I found myself trying to pray harder to protect everything and stop the leaks. I forgave God for not protecting us. I forgave myself and repented for thinking that...

Early one morning, the Lord asked me if He could talk to me. I, of course, said He could. He began by addressing a situation that had happened the night before when I read a post on Facebook where someone was asking for suggestions of retreat speakers. I wanted to write my name down in the comments, but did not because that would be weird and wrong. There was this little place inside of me that wanted to be picked and noticed. I know He is in control of where and when I speak, but there was a part of me that did not trust Him. Somehow I was thinking that He was forgetting about me. I love to teach at retreats. I love to teach. So, He told me to submit that to Him. He told me to trust Him with that. Every time it comes up, submit it to Him.

He then, went on to tell me that I was entering into a season of submission. Instead of praying for my family, our finances, our future and all the other things and people I was praying for, I was to submit them to Him. Submission was trust. As I submit, I am handing each of these to Him and trusting Him with them. It seems obvious, but what had happened was that my prayers had become fear based and not faith based. I would pray at the end of the day trying to protect my family in every way possible. When something went wrong, I was taking responsibility for not praying enough. It was twisted. In a way, the inside of me was thinking that God would perform according to my prayers or lack of prayer. If I prayed harder, situations would change. If I prayed longer, He would recognize me. It was twisted and I was not aware of it.

He was now going to show me who He was without me being involved through prayer. I was going to recognize His hand in my life without my prayers. He wants me to disconnect my responsibility in prayer to His taking care of what is important to me. I am going to learn a whole new way to pray and trust. I am going to get to experience God being my Dad and taking care of me, and I will know that it is fully Him and not because I prayed. I did not realize I was doing this until He asked me to stop praying and to submit everything to Him. I will be totally honest; I was not sure how to pray or what to do after I submitted each thing to Him. I discovered what my prayers had become...

Somehow, in the struggles of life, my prayers had turned into responsibility instead of faith. I felt I had to pray to protect my family. I felt I had to pray about our finances and my ministry or God was going to overlook me and forget. When He asked me to just submit it all to Him, I discovered what my prayers consisted of. When He takes care of something, I am going to learn that He is there for me and that He has not forgotten about me. I am going to experience His love and care. I am very excited about this...it is not the answer I thought I was praying for, but it is definitely a much bigger and deeper experience than I could have ever asked for.

If God asked you to stop praying, how would you feel about that? Is there fear? Or do you trust that He will take care of you and your family regardless of your prayers? For me, this has now freed up my time for more conversations with the Lord. This does not mean that my prayers did not matter, but He revealed what I was doing with them. I am going to submit each thing to God, and learn and be healed of my past in the process. Can you see how my prayers were becoming performance based? Ask the Lord to evaluate your prayer life...make sure you listen...

CHAPTER 15
Extras

There is so much more to prayer than what I have written about; here are a few more areas to just touch on...

Prayer and Fasting...

I have been in seasons where I did fast and pray to get breakthrough. I do not do this all the time, but as the Lord encourages me. When He asks me to do it, it is very effective for breakthrough in some areas for others and for myself. Jesus did address it in Matthew 17:21, "However, this kind does not go out except by prayer and fasting." You can read more about it in Matthew 17, if you are interested. I will admit that fasting is not my favorite thing to do, but I will obey when He asks. I have also found fasting to be effective to change habits or known idols, whether it is eating or something that is difficult to let go of. It will redirect your focus. For those who are married, it is important to have agreement with your spouse when you are fasting.

Going places or having people speak to you while in prayer...

I have encountered this many times, as did the disciples in the Bible. I did not write a chapter on it because it is not as common. But I have had moments in prayer where a mom is holding up a yearbook pointing to her son and so I pray for him. I have found myself places I have not physically been but have spiritually gone there. If this happens to you and you would like more understanding, send me an email and we can correspond that way. I only write this here to point out that it does happen in prayer to some people.

Praying in tongues or in the Spirit or a prayer language...

It is briefly mentioned in the chapter, Praying for Others. Not everyone has this experience. I do not know why. I did not ask for this gift, but I got it one evening in church. I, personally, have found it to be very helpful. Like I stated in the chapter, it is not a public speaking in tongues, but private. It is my prayer language. I have found that in some situations it changes, depending on the warfare I am praying through. At the beginning, I thought it was odd, but now I find it incredibly valuable in my prayer life. There are many opinions about this area of prayer, and for that reason, there is not a whole chapter on it. If you have more questions about it, email me and we can talk about it.

Visions and Dreams

He will communicate to us through visions and dreams, which I see as another form of prayer. Sometimes I will ask Him something and I will get an answer back in the form of a picture or vision, or even a dream. A vision can be a quick flash of something, or it can be a long experience. Learn to pay attention to how He communicates back to you. Keep a journal handy and write them down. There are times when I am praying for someone and I will get a picture or vision for them or about them. He used them in His Word all the time to give direction, instruction, and understanding...

Prophetic Words

I have found there are times when I am praying for someone, and as I am praying, I am getting a word from the Lord for the person. How do I know this? I know because it is clear understanding or direction that I gained while praying, and I had no prior thoughts like this before I prayed. This also happens when I am just speaking to someone.

Prayer is communication between God and us. He knows how to get information to us; we just need to learn how He is doing it. I hope and pray that this book has opened your eyes further into the amazing world of prayer...

"If My people who are called by My name will humble themselves, and pray and seek My face, and turn from their wicked ways, then I will hear from heaven, and will forgive their sin and heal their land" (2 Chronicles 7:14).

Do You Need Jesus?

If, for some reason, you have received this book and you do not know Jesus as your personal Savior, I want you to know that you can. Are you curious about this conversation I am talking about in this book? Do you want to experience it? If yes, then I want you to know that there is nothing you have done that He will not forgive, if you ask Him. Just say this simple prayer to begin your amazing journey with Jesus...

Dear Jesus,

Thank You for loving me and for dying on the cross for me. I ask that You please forgive me of my sins and that You come into my heart. I need You and want to get to know You. I want the love You came to give. Show me who You are. I want to love You.

In Jesus' name. Amen.

It is that simple.
Welcome to the family of God!

May I encourage you to please get connected with a local church family that will help you learn more about what you have just done. If you do not know of one, please contact me and I will help you find one.

About the Author

Cheryl Stasinowsky is a speaker and writer of passion and transparency. Her desire is for others to see Jesus in everything they walk through; growing a new passion for His Word and its relevance for them. Please contact her to make arrangements for your future events, retreats, church services, meetings, and conferences.

She would love to meet you!

cheryl@wordscribeministries.com
www.wordscribeministries.com
www.hishiddentreasure.blogspot.com

Connect with Cheryl on Facebook and twitter @histreasures

What others are saying:

"Cheryl Stasinowsky is a treasure. Cheryl is a special artist that paints her teachings in faith constructionism, and as such, she passionately extracts the blueprints from the foundation of the Word and then builds that foundation into the details of everyday practical life. Her books and teachings are a life guide, and her speaking appearances are personal. She opens herself to each person she is teaching, and lays out in honesty her own personal experiences of the presence of God within the joys and pains of everyday life."

More Titles by Cheryl Stasinowsky

His Hidden Treasures
ISBN: 978-0-6158979-9-8

There is an unknown treasure sitting on your night stand, bookshelf or coffee table. It is full of keys that will unlock your destiny, vision and purpose. They are yours for the taking. Join Cheryl on this journey as she uncovers valuable secrets found in the Bible. Through her own brokenness and surrender, the author will inspire you to embark on your own journey of searching for the timeless and endless treasures in the Word of God. As you dig deeper, each hidden treasure will leave you desperate for more of God's Word.

Deeper Relevance
ISBN: 978-0-6159069-9-7

Cheryl set out to write a daily encouraging word on her social networks, not realizing that her pursuit for a deeper understanding of God's Word would blossom into a full devotional. Grab your Bible, along with this book, and get ready to discover kingdom nuggets that will enrich your walk and relationship with Jesus. His Word truly sustains us every day!

More Titles by Cheryl Stasinowsky

Now Faith
ISBN: 978-0-615899-07-7

Now Faith is a face-to-face encounter with the men and women of Hebrews 11 who had the kind of faith that pleased God and moved mountains. Each chapter steps inside their lives, takes a look around, finds vital parts of the DNA of their faith, and then supplies a prayer for the impartation of that faith.

Now Faith in Spanish (Es Pues, La Fe)
ISBN: 978-0-615899-67-1

Es Pues, La Fe es un encuentro, cara a cara, con los hombres y mujeres de Hebreos 11 quienes tuvieron la fe que agradó a Dios y que movió montañas. Cada capítulo toma un paso adentro de sus vidas, echa un vistazo a su forma de ser, encuentra partes vitales del ADN de su fe, y después suple una oración para la impartición de esa fe.

More Titles by Cheryl Stasinowsky

Private Moments With God
ISBN: 978-0-6159103-7-6

Life as we individually know it ... Each of us has a past that is influencing how we see our present. We walk through our day with all of the pressures and demands of life with a past, in the present, and also with a hope for a future. I, too, journey this thing called life. Through it all, I have come to value to the highest degree the first moments of my early mornings when the house is quiet, it is still dark outside, my coffee is freshly brewed, my iPod is playing worship music in my ears, and I open the Word of God for my nourishment and encouragement for the day. These are those moments ...

Given to Forgive
ISBN: 978-0-692306-60-4

Are you tired of wrestling with regret, guilt, anger, resentment, bitterness, and impatience? Did you know that all of these are symptoms of unforgiveness? I did not like to forgive and always thought that the other person had to come to me first to apologize. I held onto unforgiveness for years. Eight years ago, I started forgiving people, situations, and choices I had made. I hand you my journey of choosing to be given to forgive every day...

More Titles by Cheryl Stasinowsky

Given to Love
ISBN: 978-0-692485-51-4

It is not going to be what you think it is going to be. This is not a book on love as the world sees and shows love. This is a book on my journey through discovering how to love from His word working in and through me. I have purposed to try to put on His word and live love. I am still learning, but what I have learned, I give. It has been tested and tried and has hurt a lot. I have submitted to Him in difficult situations and have chosen to walk as He showed me and not how my flesh wanted to respond ... I am Given to Love first over being right ... Love wins!

Coming soon ...

GIVEN TO CHANGE

GIVEN TO LISTEN

All of Cheryl's books are available in
eBook and print versions on Amazon and Barnes & Noble.

www.ingramcontent.com/pod-product-compliance
Lightning Source LLC
Chambersburg PA
CBHW071304040426
42444CB00009B/1868